You've Got This!

I hope you enjoy my story.

Diane King

Diane King, RN

PAGE PUBLISHING, INC.
New York, NY

First originally published by Page Publishing, Inc. 2019

ISBN 978-1-64544-358-2 (Paperback)
ISBN 978-1-64544-360-5 (Digital)

Printed in the United States of America

Introduction

It is my hope, in writing this book and sharing my journey with you, that you will take the time that is needed to help you recover from a significant loss. My husband, Marty, passed away unexpectedly from sudden cardiac arrest while we were out of town celebrating his brother's birthday in 2017. We were together for twenty-four years.

In my line of work, we see death often, unfortunately. I work as a registered nurse in a busy community hospital in Northern California in an emergency department. I have a lot to share about my experience with grieving and hope you will benefit from the knowledge I will share with you.

Before I began my nursing career, my first clear experience with loss was when I was eighteen years old. My maternal grandmother passed away, and it was a very sad time for my family and me. Shortly following, my remaining grandparents passed away (my paternal grandfather had passed away before my three brothers and I were born). My brothers and I had no living grandparents left to share in the joys of our family life together. Today I feel so happy when I see different generations together doing activities as a family.

CHAPTER 1

My Life Story

I GREW UP IN A small town in the Bay Area of California and attended a Catholic elementary school. The Sisters of the Presentation taught us that service to others was of great importance. Many of my classmates have continued to serve others in some capacity of volunteer work, trying to improve the community in which they live. Most of us are still in touch with one another, and we try to get together often and catch up when we can almost fifty-plus years later. We compare stories, and we share photos of cakes we decorated as taught to us as an after-school activity many years ago. We also took a flower-arranging class taught after school by one of the moms who also owned a local flower shop. It was a fun childhood for us.

I did not follow the traditional route of attending college after high school graduation but married young, which did not work out. What did work out was two beautiful daughters who have been a blessing to me. As a single mother of two children, I worked very hard so that they might also attend a Catholic elementary school as well. My life focus was dedicated to raising my daughters and helping them navigate through life's challenges and, eventually, helping them become strong, independent women.

The turning point for me in that relationship that was the deciding factor to end it with their father was when I went back to school part-time, many years ago, to take classes for the nursing program, and I became very ill. I was diagnosed with stage IV non-Hodgkin's lymphoma. I had to take a year off from the nursing program and focus on my health. During this time away from school, I knew I had to get better and get out of the dysfunctional relationship that I was in. I did not want my daughters brought up in a type of environment where they would think it was okay to live with someone who was not respectful to women. This was the driving force within me. I read a lot of books and gathered as much information as I could about getting my health back. Slowly, I got better. On the days I knew were going to be difficult ones after chemo, I would stock up on juice packs that small children could easily open on their own. I still clearly remember lying on the couch in my late twenties and my two young daughters bringing me something to drink. The chemotherapy regimen that was only supposed to last three months turned into six months as I could not recover rapidly enough between treatments to be treated the following week. It was an aggressive treatment plan, and there are newer medications now that help with this.

My nursing-school friends, each and every one of them, supported me in some way, whether it was driving me to treatments, helping with my children, or bringing a meal over. The love and support were overwhelming. For my final doctor visit in 1988, my mother had driven me up to Stanford Hospital, and as we were leaving, I placed a call from the pay phone near the hospital exit door to call the father of my children to tell him that the treatments were all done and there was no clinical detection of any cancer cells in my body. His response to me was "Good, can I leave you now?" I looked over at my mother, smiled sweetly, said "Thank you for your support" to him, and hung up. I never said a word to my mother about what had transpired. I knew then and there that I had to get out. My mother had no idea of the hell I was living in. The situation was bad enough for all of us, and I could not deliver one more blow to either of my parents by letting them know how horrible my home life was, so I endured it until I could graduate from nursing school and support myself and my two daughters.

As I was approaching graduation in the spring of 1990, a group of my clinical students would get together on Saturdays to study in Downtown San Jose at SJSU (San Jose State University). We had it all figured out. We decided beforehand who would bring which textbook along as we only needed one book to study with per course. The textbooks were probably three inches thick, and we had several courses that we were taking our finals in. It was backbreaking to try to carry three or four textbooks that were heavy across the campus for all of us. Our plan worked well for us and got us through school.

One Saturday, I had just locked my car and started walking toward the library with my backpack when I noticed a lot of commotion down the street I was walking on. It was a father and mother panicking, yelling, and screaming while carrying a limp toddler who was turning blue. They were in obvious distress, and I could not ignore what was going on. They did not speak English, but I did tell them I could help them. It was clear the child had choked on something obstructing his airway. I gently took the toddler and administered back blows and abdominal thrusts, enough to create a partial airway, which took less than one minute. The child's color improved, and he became conscious. I used their phone to call 911 immediately. When the 911 dispatcher answered, I was completely surprised to recognize the voice I heard. It was one of my best friends, Cheryl. I explained to her that we needed an ambulance for a child with a partially obstructed airway and that the child was now breathing but compromised. I waited for the ambulance to arrive, and they were able to remove a partially chewed grape from the child's airway using Magill forceps. They transported the patient to the hospital, and he was admitted for observation. I was late meeting my clinical group but glad I was able to help save a child's life.

When I graduated from nursing school, the director of nurses asked me if I could get ahold of the family of this child and have them come to our graduation. I didn't want to make a big deal out of it and told her it wasn't necessary. I just wanted to get through graduation and start studying for the NCLEX exam for nurses. At graduation, there were two awards given to the students, one was academic and one was the Perseverance Award. I was awarded the Perseverance Award and was so honored to receive this. It meant a lot to me, but I could not have done it without all the love and support from my fellow students. I am still grateful to this day and keep in touch with my core clinical group that began with me in the late 1980s. I graduated, passed the NCLEX exam on the first try, and already had a job offer waiting at the local community hospital in the emergency department.

I then slowly began telling my parents of the circumstances that I was in, and they did all that they could to help me. My first job after being hired was working the night shift, and my parents would often care for my children as I worked. My brothers also helped me as much as they could between their own jobs and attending college themselves. It somehow all worked out, and we got through it. I graduated, owned a home, found a well-paying job and did well. I also picked up a second job along the way with Holland America cruise line as a ship nurse. It was an exciting job that took me to the Caribbean, Alaska (a couple of times), Russia, and the Baltic region. The great thing about the nursing profession is all the facets it has to offer. My favorite facet of the nursing profession is in the emergency department.

There are many certifications that emergency nurses must maintain at minimum. Emergency nurses are ACLS (advanced cardiac life support)–certified. I initially took this course in 1991 and have recertified fourteen times, most recently two weeks prior to my husband's sudden death.

When Marty died, he had just dropped his brother off at his hotel and was on his way back to our hotel room. Marty was alone when he went into sudden cardiac arrest and died. He was not found for hours. The AHA (American Heart Association) protocol for sudden cardiac arrest is defibrillation, and that could have saved his life, if witnessed. Processing a sudden death is difficult.

In retrospect, death and dying affects everyone at some point in their life. I felt that when I became seriously ill, I had no choice but to fight as hard as I could to survive, not only for myself but also for my family. Plus, my job was just beginning. I finished my chemotherapy regimen and was put in remission with no guarantees of nonrecurrence given, similar to living with a gun to your head. As time progressed, my chance of recurrence became less likely.

I knew that I was not done yet. I had to give back. I volunteered for the United Way Role Model Program speaking to at-risk youth and talking to them about the importance of staying in school. I met with students at the assigned schools and spoke about becoming a nurse and how many lives I affected, not only in nursing school but also on the job. On this one day, Marty agreed to join me and be a spectator. I felt like I was not connecting at all for the first time with the students as most of the students that day were early teenage boys. I think they had lost interest in hearing about the rewards of the nursing profession. Marty was in the back, and I invited him to come up and speak.

"Hey yo! How you guys all doing today? Did you catch that game last weekend? What a play, huh?" I saw the look of disinterest turn into intense listening skills, and Marty was holding a captive audience. Marty was talking to them about becoming a police officer and how many people that he had helped. He had many stories he had to tell. The students became more interested and were raising their hands and asking questions about how he became a police officer, and he answered them. Soon our time was up and they had to get back to class, but I have never forgotten that day and how Marty's charismatic personality stole the show. I was so glad he had come with me.

I also joined the JLSJ (Junior League of San Jose) in 1988 and began my volunteer hours working on a project called LACY (Legal Advocates for Children and Youth). This project helped establish guardianships and helped prevent minors from entering the foster care system. I worked on a project called Kids in the Kitchen. This project is grounded in the belief that children and families empowered with the knowledge of how to feed and exercise their bodies will be less likely to become obese and, subsequently, suffer the many associated health risks. I also served on the board of directors for JLSJ and had the opportunity to learn about nonprofit organizations and the business aspect of giving back to the community.

My favorite project with the JLSJ was the GCRP (Grandparent Caregiver Resource Program). The GCRP assists older adults caring for a grandchild in their own home when the parents are unavailable. The goal is to ease the burden an older adult may have when raising a family member's children. I was on the committee for a year and then served as the committee chair. I am now a sustainer and, most recently, was the sustaining adviser to the annual fund-raiser, in which all proceeds are distributed back to the local community. The beneficiaries of the proceeds for the local nonprofit agencies are voted on by the board of directors based on need.

After being employed at the hospital for a few years, I began working toward my clinical ladder promotion and was able to apply some of the community service that I had done in addition to working on hospital committees, participating in research projects, taking additional continued-education courses above and beyond what was required, working on department projects, and becoming nationally certified in emergency nursing. The requirement was to obtain ten points from various activities to qualify. I had acquired twenty-six points. I was nominated for the Frist Humanitarian Award by a coworker and was awarded this honor. The Frist Humanitarian Award is a tribute to Dr. Frist's lifelong dedication to improving the lives of others. Each year, this award recognizes individuals at the hospital who demonstrate a level of commitment and caring that goes beyond everyday kindness. I still love bedside nursing and have no interest in working on the management side. I help when I can with the annual skills validation, but my heart is in working directly with the patients. Many of my friends are also nurses, and they enjoy dealing with people and working with the community.

My high school friends and I were discussing a way to pay it forward and a way to create a fund-raiser so that we could gift a financial scholarship from our class to a graduating senior from our high school. We were approaching our fortieth high school reunion in 2017. There were four of us on the planning committee, and we met several times to discuss how we could accomplish this. We decided that we could create a cookbook with recipes from our classmates and sell it to the public at a reasonable cost.

I gathered family-favorite recipes together from our classmates, edited them, and compiled them into a cookbook. We set up a screening questionnaire, interviews, worked with the academic counselor, and began the screening process. We sold out of cookbooks and had enough money for two students to receive a scholarship! It was very moving to read the thank-you letters from the recipients at our reunion. We are in the process of brainstorming what we can accomplish next.

My father was a great influence on volunteering and giving back to the community and was involved with local organizations as we were growing up, such as the Kiwanis Club and Elks Club. I remember him helping to build local parks in our community and taking pride in the work that was done to improve our town.

My parents have now both passed away—both from pancreatic cancer, ironically. We used the hospice program for both of them. I took a leave of absence to help care for both of them during their time of need. I feel grateful that I was able to help. They were both in their familiar surroundings, and I was able to help provide for them a death with dignity in their own home, surrounded by those who love them, and in a peaceful environment.

My daughters were there helping to support and nurture them during their final hours, a great lesson to learn for them about the importance of family and being together through the good times and bad.

I am still helping my daughters through the challenges that life brings, which includes helping when I can with their families as they now are both happily married and have three children of their own. Their story is much different than how my story initially started out to be as they have both been blessed with the best husbands/fathers I could have ever asked for, for both of them and their families.

 Some things to consider: Journaling your thoughts can be therapeutic, especially reflecting back and seeing the progress and how far you have come. If journaling is not your cup of tea, perhaps drawing or photographing might help you.

CHAPTER 2

Putting All My Eggs in One Basket

MY NEIGHBOR FROM MY OLD neighborhood across the street also helped me during the week. I would pay her for my children to spend the night while I worked. I would iron their little uniforms and make their lunch the night before, and then I would come home the next morning and drive them to school then go home and sleep. We had a great pattern and made it work. One day, my neighbor mentioned that her single brother was coming over and that he was a police sergeant and asked if I would like to join them for dinner. I politely told her that I was not interested in meeting anyone, especially a law enforcement officer. So many would often come into my workplace, and I simply was not interested. But certainly, I would stop by to say hello to meet her family. She also told me that he had also attended Catholic school, like I did, and went on to play football in college at USC and helped win the national championship at USC as their punter in 1978.

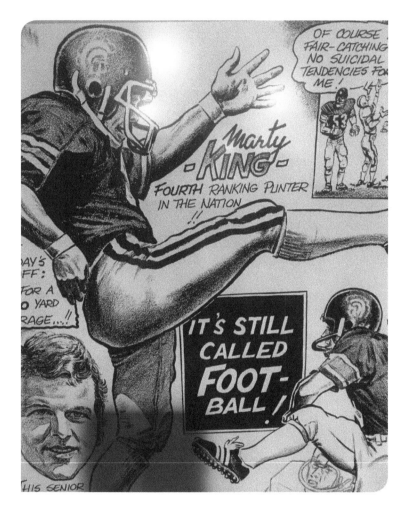

The day came around for me to make the trip across the street to finally meet the famous Uncle Marty, also known as UM. He was not what I expected at all. In front of me was the kindest, warm-hearted man that I had ever met. There was no macho cop persona about him whatsoever. I would not have ever picked him out of a crowd to be in the law enforcement profession, with all due respect to police officers, of course. Here was this well-spoken gentle giant asking how my day was and wanting to hear about my profession. He let me know that his mother was also a registered nurse and that he took a particular interest in nurses and what a noble profession nursing is. I thanked him for a nice evening and told him what a pleasure it was to meet him.

He called a few days later and asked if I would be interested in going to lunch with him next time he was in town. I thought about it and agreed. "Sure, why not?" We went to a nice coastal restaurant and spent the afternoon beachside talking about life in general. Next, he invited me to dinner and dancing after at a lovely restaurant nearby. I knew that night he was the one I wanted to spend the rest of my life with. I told him that I thought I was falling in love with him.

He called me every day since our first date in 1993, wherever in the world I was. We spoke for twenty-four years. Many times it was several calls or text messages during the day. In the nineties, when pagers were in, he would page me "143" throughout the day, letting me know how much he loved me. We had talked openly of spending the rest of our lives together and eventually getting married. However, we were both in no hurry to take the giant step into marriage.

Marty, at the time, lived about five hours away in Southern California. One night, while on duty, he had suffered a significant hearing loss when responding to a call where a psychiatric patient had attempted to harm himself with a shotgun, and the blast was very close to Marty, which later resulted in a medical retirement from law enforcement after seventeen years of service. He eventually relocated back to the Bay Area.

After packing up his belongings, we had agreed to meet in Las Vegas, and I would then drive home with him back to the Bay Area, which was before we owned cell phones. I flew into McCarran

Airport and waited and waited. I did not realize at that time that I needed to take a tram to the terminal and thought that I had been ditched. I was so upset that I began thinking about rebooking a flight back home. In order to do that, I needed to take the tram back to the terminal to speak to an agent. As I stepped off the tram, Marty was standing there patiently waiting for me and quite worried. "Where have you been?" I was so happy to see him but yet still so angry because I had believed that I had been ditched for good! Again, it all worked out.

Marty realized it was time to start a second career and decided to attend law school and become a criminal defense attorney, which was a four-year process. He served on the law review board and received numerous awards during school and excelled in the evidence class and criminal procedure, which he had an extensive background in. He also helped other classmates to understand the tough curriculum. Law school graduation came and went, and it was now time to study for the state bar exam. He was not successful on the first try and knew what he had to do to pass this tough exam. Six months later, he went to Sacramento, California, to take the three-day exam, and I told him that I would meet him in the Reno/Tahoe area when he was all done and we could celebrate! All he could focus on after day 3 was driving up to meet me and unwind from all the stress. We had a fantastic time and celebrated. Months later, he came over to check the results that were to be published on the internet that November. He logged on at his assigned time, and I recall seeing tears form in his eyes for the first time ever. "I passed."

The following April was his birthday, and he asked if I would like to go and celebrate with him in Carmel at the Highlands Inn. I willing agreed. As we sat down to dinner, I toasted him and wished him a happy birthday, and he took a small box out of his jacket and told me that I would really make his birthday special if I said yes. I knew that, eventually, we would get married but was shocked that he had proposed and had it all figured out—the ring, the timing, etc. What a beautiful evening we had together—the view of the ocean, quiet atmosphere, and our whole life ahead of us. During one of many long talks, he talked about the synonym of never putting "all of your eggs in one basket." In other words, he meant "to totally rely on someone or something." I could not help but put all my eggs in one basket when it came to him. I truly saw no other way but growing old together with him. He was all I ever wanted in one big package. It was all I ever dreamed of. There was not one thing he could have ever done to change my opinion of him, ever.

 It may help you to make a movie of your favorite pictures or to simply gather photographs and put them in a special box to look at when you feel the need to reminisce.

CHAPTER 3

Making Time to "Get Off the Grid"

ONE OF OUR FAVORITE VACATION spots in the world has always been Hawaii. We loved Maui, Oahu, Kona, and Kauai each individually for different reasons—Maui for the beautiful beaches and the time-share we own there, Oahu for the fabulous restaurant choices and choice of city life and/or calming lagoons where we would stay in Ko Olina, Kona for the rural aspect, and last but not least, Kauai. Marty loved Hanalei Bay. He could float for hours out on the bay, looking at the ocean and then looking the other way to see the beautiful waterfalls. It was in Princeville that he discovered his beloved "hula dogs," which is a hot dog or sausage wrapped in a cone-shaped grilled device with lilikoi mustard. I purchased a hula dog machine for him when we came home, and he enjoyed his attempts to replicate their famous mustard sauces for everyone to try. When he discovered a local shop that sold these hot dog concoctions, he proudly wore his "U of H" hat into the store, hoping they would comment on his hat. And of course they did, much to his joy.

One of our favorite things was to make a picnic and go to the beach and just relax while, of course, bringing his favorite collapsible cooler. We always wished we had more time to do this.

We had fun vacations together in Sedona, New Orleans, Lake Tahoe, Reno, San Diego; and we had so many happy memories and stories to relive over and over again—laughing, dancing, living life to the fullest.

Some things to consider: Write a letter to your loved one, and let them know how much you enjoyed the time spent together and your favorite memories together.

CHAPTER 4

The Power Couple

WE HAD A SMALL INTIMATE wedding in 2001, and we invited a small group of family and friends and went to the Reno/Tahoe area on our honeymoon.

I often helped Marty in his job as a criminal defense attorney as his expert witness, testifying in court or at the DMV hearings in matters that required medical expert opinion. I did not mind at all and helped explain the medical terminology that was often complex and difficult for a lay person to understand. This came easily for me as I do contract work for the California Board of Registered Nurses in Sacramento, working with the department of consumer affairs as an expert witness; and this was very similar work. I also became a notary public at his request, in the event he needed items notarized from his law office.

How Marty helped me in my career at the hospital was helping me write reports for our emergency department that were succinct. He was an excellent writer and could easily write a letter without much thought beforehand, which would take hours if I wrote it—just in revisions on my behalf. In addition, he was a gadget wizard and could set up all our computers, home-theater devices, sound systems, and any electronic devices. I can recall numerous times pleading with him, "Please help me with the printer. It is just not printing." I would promise, "This will be the last time today that I will bother you to help me. Well, maybe, I might ask again in five minutes. Let's just see how I will do, okay?" He would, on several occasions, stop whatever he was doing, look at me, shake his head, get up, and fix it for me, mumbling that I really need to figure this all out. Meanwhile, I was sticking Post-it notes on everything: "UM said to load the paper this way" or "UM said to scan the documents upside down." The Post-it notes are still there to this day.

We had a synergistic relationship. When we hosted our parties, he would take care of the main course, whether it was barbecuing or smoking the meat; and I would create the side dishes and dessert, order the invitations, create the centerpieces, and set a beautiful table.

I have fifteen sets of dishes and used them all for different occasions. One of my favorite things to do for Marty was make a themed dinner and welcome him home to a candlelit dinner with Pandora playing in the background. It would be playing whatever the theme was—French served with beef bourguignon, Italian with a multitude of dishes, Zydeco with a New Orleans–themed meal, a Hawaiian-themed dinner, Hungarian with a fragrant paprika goulash, or simple Spanish tapas. He loved it all and was so happy I took the time to do this for him after a day of hard work. Sometimes I would ask him after if he remembered the dishes that I served him dinner on. Honestly, he did not always remember that part, but he could tell me how good the food tasted. I think his all-time favorite day was on Father's Day when he was sunbathing and I brought us Bloody Mary's to enjoy poolside as we lounged in the pool.

When Marty's father became ill and was no longer able to drive, a caretaker was hired to care for him so that he could stay in his home environment. We had arranged through the transit system a van that could accommodate a wheelchair and for his caretaker to bring him to our home, which is about a half hour away. His father suffered from dementia later in life. On one specific occasion, I served dinner on my Franciscan plates, which consisted of meatloaf, green beans, and a baked potato. For a long time, we would recall how, for just that evening only, Marty's father became more lucid. We credit that to the familiarity of the dishes as Marty's grandmother also had Franciscan plates and often served him the same meal. When Marty's father looked at him and said, "How are you doing, Marty?" he was in awe. His father had not looked directly to him and spoken to him in months. He reverted back into his state of dementia shortly after.

Imagine your favorite place to relax and be alone, whether sitting at a beach or in the middle of a forest—really, anything works. What would you say to your loved one? What would you imagine they would say to you?

CHAPTER 5

The Family Dynamics

As MENTIONED EARLIER, IT WAS so important to me that I raise my daughters to become strong independent women and eventually be in healthy, loving relationships. Marty and I both witnessed years of heartache, tears, and letdowns of many wrong characters who passed through our home over many years, often referred to as "Johnny's" as Marty could not remember their names long enough to matter and some were not welcomed back.

Marty taught both of my daughters how to drive a car and eventually gave them his old T-bird. They would laugh when they heard him coming around the corner with the music blaring, brakes screeching, and sunflower seeds flying out the window. They often took their friends joyriding in his car, with his permission, of course; and they would giggle at all the sunflower seeds flying around the car and the tattered interior upholstery, which all added character. They were all truly Marty's girls. He always took the time to talk to each of their friends and ask them how their day was going.

One of the projects that he undertook at my home was mowing the lawn. It would take him longer to gear up to do this than to actually mow the lawn itself. The lawn area was probably ten by ten feet. Marty would don a tank top, wear his shorts and tennis shoes, put on his earbuds, and last but not least, his do-rag. Of course, finding the right music to play took up most of the time. An hour later, the lawn looked beautiful. I never said a word. I was just so happy that he took care of it for me. We would all line up just to watch him in action at his finest, rocking out to whatever jam he had going.

He was always so thoughtful like that. He knew I was tired and helped a lot. Once, while vacuuming, I realized what time it actually was, turned the vacuum off in the center of the room, and rushed out the door to pick up my children from school. When I returned home, Marty had stopped by, saw that I had not finished vacuuming, completed it for me, and put the vacuum away. I was stunned that he actually did that. He was always so thoughtful. That was the kind of man that I wanted my daughters to find someday.

Eventually, both of my daughters married thoughtful men who were also college athletes and who also happened to be in law enforcement. The standing joke often retold was when both of the sons-in-law had asked Marty for a beer, and in typical Marty fashion, he replied, "Sure, go help yourself." They could not find it, and Marty laughed, telling them, "You call yourselves investigators but cannot find the beer that is in the refrigerator?" He got many miles out of that one for sure. He had to get up and show them where the beer was stashed, shaking his head the entire time.

When our first grandchild, Addison, was born in 2009, it changed our world. Marty now had a new buddy to play the piano with, have tea parties with, and go searching for bugs with. And his most favorite was that he now had a swimming pal on Friday afternoons. He would schedule his calendar as to not interfere with his standing Friday afternoon date in the spring and summer of swimming with Addison. He would teasingly tell her she was being a pest with a capital *P*! The more he told her that, the more egged on she would become. He had no peace, but he loved every minute of swimming, splashing, sunbathing, floating around, and just enjoying his life.

Another role he assumed was, on the days he did not have court early, he would take pride in driving her to school. He would come back home and tell me that she just "jabbered" the entire time. He loved it. He knew all her friends and teachers and what was happening at school. Addison loved the beef jerky that Marty would make her for her lunch, and she said she would not share. It was that special.

Marty and I enjoyed barbecuing and smoking a variety of meats and often would reflect back on the water smoker that I purchased for him in 2001, which progressed into much bigger and better smokers with several state-of-the-art gadgetry that accompanied his smoker systems. I suggested to one of his friends that I had a proposition for the both of them, and they wondered what I had to offer. There was a local barbecue competition that I thought they may be interested in. They both loved it and started competition barbecue. I got a certification in food preparation through our county, and we both became KCBS (Kansas City Barbecue Society) judges. The competition barbecue did not last long as it took a great deal of time to prepare for, was expensive, and took a lot of cleanup. Marty much preferred to cook for family and friends and not be judged on his culinary expertise. He also began making sausage and packaging it up for family and friends to enjoy.

What was your loved one's favorite food? Have you considered making their favorite meal and sharing it with friends or coworkers for a special occasion?

CHAPTER 6

Living the Healthy Lifestyle

OUR HANDS DOWN FAVORITE MEAL during the summertime was caprese salad, and we had that during the summer at least twice a week and never tired of it. We grew the tomatoes and the basil ourselves in our garden. We would make the salad together, laughing and talking about our day, and have a cocktail while we typically watched the evening news and enjoyed our salad. We did try to eat healthy, but there were countless times that I did hear the microwave go off after I went to bed. Quite simply, Marty loved to eat and enjoy good food. Being a master BBQ expert, it was not always red meat or pork. Often he would smoke fish to enjoy and package it up to freeze.

One day, he said, "I am not feeling right. My vision is blurry, I can't focus well, and I cannot get enough water. As fast as I am drinking it, I have to urinate." I made a phone call to a friend that had a home glucometer and asked if I might borrow it.

The glucose reading was 458. I immediately called his primary-care physician and asked to him please make time for us that afternoon. We met him at his office and agreed that the best course of treatment was to get his glucose under control in the hospital. During this time, it was flu season, and I pleaded with his doctor to not admit him and that I would care for him at home. Every four hours, I would check his glucose around the clock until we could slowly get his blood sugar to a reasonable range.

We closely monitored his glucose level throughout the day for two weeks and eventually tapered down to twice-per-day checks. He was finally able to come off regular insulin and control his glucose level with oral medication. He struggled with admitting that he had type 2 diabetes. He would try to convince me that he was not a diabetic anymore, and I countered with "Yes, you are still a diabetic, but you should be able to control it with proper medication and diet." This did not go over well at all.

Marty's favorite things to cook for our family was smoked beef brisket, pork baby back ribs, pulled pork, or tri-tip. When we had a BBQ at our home and people were invited, we rarely got a no on the RSVP, and if we did, it was usually because someone would be out of town. Our B-list group was not included on many occasions unless it was a large party. The food that he prepared was that good.

He loved fresh vegetables, and our meals were not complete without them. He also had a salad nightly, and his weekly meal prep usually consisted of marinated cucumbers with sliced onion, chopped smoked chicken, grilled vegetables, and pretoasted bread for a turkey sandwich with a dill pickle. On Sunday, he would prepare for his week by grilling away and watching sports on his outdoor TV.

Let's be real here. Often, I would find wrappers in his car from convenience stores and quick stops from a spicy fried burrito, candy bars, or chips. I would not be honest in this writing if I did not mention Marty's shortcomings and his love of food.

From the day that I met Marty, he was an exercise fanatic, and at minimum, he would exercise three times per week. He had a club membership and would alternate using the gym with the equipment that we had purchased in our home—a cross trainer, a treadmill, and a stationary bicycle. He would put his headset on, use his playlist, and sweat up a storm for at least forty-five minutes. I never would have imagined that he had health problems as severe as he actually did, demonstrated by his physical strength. I kept telling myself that he was doing well for age sixty. I could not go for forty-five minutes nonstop using the settings and incline that he selected when he worked out. Things couldn't be too bad if he could do that, right?

I would jokingly tell him, if he reached for seconds of anything, "Please remember that you are not at training table any longer from your college football days. It is harder to lose those pounds now than before!" And then he would usually begin with a story about how hard they worked out then, going to the Los Angeles Coliseum and running the stairs with the other team players.

I would often ask him if he would go with me on a long walk and we could bring the dog and all get in some exercise together—a win-win, right? There was no way that he would go with me on a walk. I think maybe he accompanied me only once, and that was most likely because he lost a bet. He felt that walking was for old people, and there was no flexibility in his decision. So I ventured out on walks with neighbors or friends or alone with our dog.

Marty excelled at any sport that he played. Early on in elementary school, he played basketball and was usually the top-scoring team member. Even though he played football in college and professionally, his favorite sport was baseball, both watching and playing it. I am saddened that I never got the opportunity to actually watch him play football or baseball. He played both football in high school as the quarterback and baseball in high school as the pitcher. We took the girls to the batting cages when they were in high school, but that was the extent of my observation. He also played golf and had the longest drive that I have ever seen. He would never say that he played a good game. He always had to improve something.

We met up with friends in Palm Springs and played some of the courses there, and I laughed so hard as we approached the pond. He stopped and just looked at me and said, "I love you but don't waste a ball. Just pick it up and drop it on the other side." Others may have been insulted by his comment, but I knew he was right. He knew me so well. Plus, I bought the pretty hot-pink golf balls and really did not want to take a chance in losing my ball! So I happily dropped the ball on the other side and continued our game. Where did that beer cart go, anyway?

Tennis is another story. When we would go to our resort in Hawaii, we always packed our athletic shoes. We did not go so far as to pack along our racquets. We borrowed them, which was fine with both of us. Marty got a run for his money when we played tennis, and he did not always come out the winner. We did play locally a few times, but that was something we always enjoyed doing in Hawaii after our coffee and before it got too hot and humid outside early in the day. He was never a sore loser, or maybe he just let me win, I'll never know. What I do know is that he was sweating harder than I was by the end of the game and he got challenged.

I was promised for twenty-four years that someday we would go to Los Angeles at the infamous USC versus UCLA game in November and he would participate in the "walk of fame" with the other former players. Each year I would ask, and each year there was a reason that we could not go. His final year, in 2017, he said he was going to make it happen that year, which fatefully never came to fruition. I was so looking forward to that experience with him and to see him in his element. Fight on!

What was your favorite healthy meal that you liked to enjoy with your loved one? What was their favorite sport to watch or participate in?

CHAPTER 7

Something Does Not Feel Right

AS WE WERE PREPARING FOR bed and had just gotten settled in, Marty looked at me and said, "You know, something is just not right." I took his pulse, and it was irregular. I inquired about chest pain, and he said it was maybe a two or three but not too bad. He denied having shortness of breath or nausea and described the quality of pain as a dull type of pain, nonradiating to his jaw or arms. I looked at him and told him that I thought we needed to go to the hospital and have him evaluated by a physician and get an EKG. He begrudgingly agreed, which surprised me. He packed a bag, and I called ahead to let my coworkers know that we were coming in for a cardiac evaluation. The EKG was not conclusive, but he was to be admitted for observation and cardiac monitoring and further studies.

I stayed in the emergency department with him for a while but getting an inpatient bed would not be until well after midnight. We both agreed that it would be a good idea for me to go home, take care of our pets, and return in the morning. After a not-so-good night's rest, I returned to the hospital, and he was sitting up in bed, ready for the next step while reading his iPad (eyeglasses on) and keeping up with the current events. "Hey, what do you say there?" He was so happy to see me, and he let me know how the night had been. He had slept well, and so we both waited for the cardiologist to arrive and see what the plan of care was.

Eventually, the cardiologist arrived, and the plan was to have an echocardiogram and a stress treadmill test. I had appointments during the day, and we agreed that I would come back that evening when I had gotten things situated at home.

I returned that evening, and the physician told us that he had an enlarged heart, also known as cardiomegaly, which caused his heart to not function properly. This was not a critical situation but it was one that needed to be observed, and he needed to stay one more night for them to monitor his heart. He was okay with the decision. Dinner arrived, and there was a look on his face when he opened the food cover. "Are you kidding me?" The look on his face was total shock. The doctor had ordered a low-sodium cardiac diet for him, which was less than 1,800 calories. It was a meatloaf slice that was probably the size of a silver dollar, a scoop of rice, and some steamed broccoli along with a nice garnishment of a fresh orchid. He took a picture of it and said, "This is just like an appetizer, just great, no salt, just salt substitute." He was so discouraged. I felt so bad for him as reality was setting in.

The following day he was getting discharged home. He was really excited and could not wait to get back to his routine, to his job, to his bed, and to just being home.

We followed up, as advised, with his physician and were told that eventually, this would be his fatality as one cannot survive with a cardiomegaly at this severity and there was no cure. On the other hand, this was not something that would happen imminently but most likely later in life. Continuous follow-up was what was recommended, and he got the green light to continue to exercise as he still needed to lose those extra pounds.

Another concern that I had about his health was that he was having allergic reactions to food that he was consuming. I started documenting exactly what he had eaten since his initial onset on October, 12th, 2011. It did not make any sense. Nothing was consistent. He was allergy tested, and the items that showed an allergen were things that he had eaten for many years—such as onions, mustard, hot dogs, mayonnaise, and cabbage—and never had an issue with. He continued to eat what he wanted, and many times he would consume these items and not have a problem. I have sixteen episodes documented. The last episode occurred six days before he died. He stopped on his way home for a pastrami sandwich with mustard. He called on his way home and said the allergic reaction was happening again and he was almost home and did not have his EpiPen in his briefcase. He arrived safely home, grabbed his EpiPen, and injected it; and the throat swelling went down right away.

As a nurse, it would be easy for me to look back in retrospect and see what I could have done differently in helping to manage his health. When he passed away suddenly and unexpectedly, I could not have changed a thing. He would have done what he wanted to do whether I was aware or not. He knew what needed to happen to maintain a healthy lifestyle.

I have told so many of my patients' family members who are feeling guilty about their loved one's hospitalization and/or death and who are saying, "If I only would have done this or done that," please do not beat yourself up for issues or circumstances. We cannot control everything. As much as we would like to, it is not always up to us. Try to focus on the positive things that you did for them. How did you impact their life? What did they love most about you?

CHAPTER 8

I Can't Thank You Enough

As WE WERE SETTLING IN for the evening, there were a few things I needed to say. Since he was diagnosed with cardiomegaly, I had been thinking about our life of twenty-four years together and what I needed to tell him. I began with thanking Marty for all he had done for my daughters and me and that he had played a key role in the success of raising such a beautiful family. Without him guiding us and leading by example how men should treat women, we would not be where we were today. He knew that and listened intently to what I had to say. I spoke from the heart and explained how much gratitude I had and spoke on behalf of both of my daughters as well. I know how much they, too, appreciated beyond words all he had done for us, stepping up to the plate as a real man. He appreciated what was said, and it meant a lot to him. That was all that was said. I said my piece and got it off my chest. He knew exactly how I felt about him and where we stood emotionally, and I am so glad that discussion happened. What regret I did hold on to for a very long time was not being able to say goodbye.

After a great deal of thought, tears, and attempts at letter writing, tearing it up and starting over again several times, I was able to let this go. It took a really long time. I resolved this nagging ache in my heart by writing a well-thought-out letter to him that I was finally satisfied with, and I was finally able to resolve my regret.

November 10, 2015

If you could share your gratitude now, what would you say to your loved one? What were you most thankful for during your time together?

CHAPTER 9

Typical Family Holiday Madness

OUR FAMILY HOLIDAY FESTIVITIES BEGIN the weekend after Thanksgiving. All the Christmas decorations get pulled out of the storage area, and it's out with some of the old and in with some of the new decorations. This is the time to repair any of the broken ornaments, glue broken decorations, and update the Christmas card list.

On this particular year, we had planned our annual get-together with Marty's Bellarmine high school friends, and I had to make good use of my time to have everything up and done before then. I had worked the day that we set our tree up, and I was feeling tired from being on my feet all day and awake since 5:00 a.m. Marty really wanted to wait and do this in a day or two, but I was on a mission to get this done. Customarily, I decorated the tree while Marty supervised, having a cocktail while we listened to Christmas music. We would reminisce about many of our ornaments that we collected along the way from our travels near and far. As I pulled out the glass string of chili pepper ornaments that we had acquired while in Sedona, I accidentally dropped them and was horrified! Marty said, "Now look at you, you are so tired that you are not even paying attention. You are like a monkey with a football. Here, let me help you!" I was so surprised that he offered to help. This simply was just not his idea of fun, and then I felt bad about rushing to get this done. He, too, enjoyed pulling the ornaments out of the box and recalling where we had visited and how much fun we had when we were there. There were ornaments from twenty-four years ago that we had acquired together. We looked at "Our first Christmas together" ornament through to the "Merry Christmas, Grandpa" ornament with a grandpa and three grandchildren from 2016.

Eventually, the outdoor lights were hung, beautifully wrapped presents were put under the tree, and the decorations were up; we were ready to start entertaining.

The first Saturday in 2016, I hosted our annual cookie exchange / luncheon with about fifteen women and filled the dining room table with a beautiful array of home-baked goodness to share with friends. Marty always made a point to make an appearance at any shower, cookie exchange, luncheon, or get-together that I hosted in our home. He would pop his head in, say hello, visit for a while, and then disappear. Eventually, all the guests left, and I needed to clean up and reset the table for our next party at five that evening with his high school friends.

Marty smoked a beautiful prime rib, I had made the side dishes and dessert beforehand, and we laughed and sipped port wine long into the evening and celebrated long friendships. Marty was always very good about pitching in and cleaning up. We both agreed that we did not like to wake up to dirty dishes to deal with, so we stayed up late getting everything done and having one last cocktail while recapping the evening.

The following day, on Sunday, we went to our grandson Chase's first birthday at noon. We had everything cleaned up from the night before and were ready to go on to our next party, but we were dragging a little by this time. He wanted to get home early so he could finish grinding the sausage that he had started so it would be ready for the smoker in a few days. He mentioned that while he was working in his cook shack, he had felt really dizzy and had to sit down. I reminded him to make sure he had his phone near him and to sit slowly if he felt dizzy and to take a break when he needed to. We could always finish it later together.

The following weekend, I was scheduled to work, but we also had a police officer academy training graduation party of a good friend that we both felt it was important to attend. We had a good time. We ran into a lot of people we had not seen for quite a while, and it was good to catch up with one another's lives.

The following week, we had three more midweek Christmas parties. By the time the third weekend arrived, we'd previously agreed to babysit our granddaughter on Saturday night so that her parents could attend a work Christmas party then on Sunday, arrive early at the hospital for a scheduled C-section for granddaughter no. 3's arrival! Midweek was the light festival show in Los Gatos, and we still had a few more days to prepare for the Christmas Eve celebration in our home with friends and family and then our traditional Christmas Day brunch in our home with just our family. Again, Marty made the main course for both meals, and I prepared the side dishes and dessert.

For Christmas that year, I was really excited about the gift that I had given Marty. it was a pair of virtual-reality binoculars that was compatible with his iPhone. He loved it and started downloading programs to watch right away.

As we started packing away the Christmas decorations, I mentioned that it would be nice if we took his brother to dinner for his birthday in January, perhaps meet him in San Francisco and spend some time with him and his new girlfriend that we had not met. He agreed and said he would get back to me after checking his schedule. It was a busy time as he was preparing for a trial. I gave it about a week as he had the tendency to procrastinate. I made reservations for the four of us in San Francisco, and Marty agreed.

New Year's came and went, which is one holiday that we were okay with staying home and not going out. I think, in twenty-four years, we went out once, and that was because Lou's Village in San Jose was closing and having a final New Year's Eve party, so we met with friends that particular year and whooped it up. We both worked with the public in our careers during New Year's and mutually agreed that the safest place for us was at home, celebrating together, and that is the reason, with one exception, that it became our tradition.

 What was your most memorable holiday together and why? Did you entertain, or did you go to family or friends or a favorite restaurant?

CHAPTER 10

The Fateful Weekend Getaway

THE WEEKEND CAME AROUND THAT we had long been waiting for—a trip out of town to celebrate the birthday of Marty's brother! I had wanted to leave early Saturday, take our time, and have a leisurely lunch in the Italian section of North Beach. Marty had a different idea. He wanted to wrap up some last-minute details for work during this three-day holiday weekend before he had court on Tuesday. He had a heavy case that was starting trial. I was disappointed but understood. Instead, we stopped for sandwiches along the way. I was careful when picking out chips with his sandwich for him. The last time he consumed jalapeño chips, he developed an allergic reaction. That was the last thing we needed as we planned on having a fun weekend ahead. I packed out Hydro Flask water bottles, a pretty nightgown to wear for Marty, and even his mother's cocktail ring, which had been passed down to me after she passed away, to wear proudly. Unfortunately, I was on the tail end of a bad sinus cold and taking a lot of anti-inflammatory medication to ease the pressure.

We had been talking on the way up to San Francisco about when he would retire as he would be turning sixty-one in a few months and wanted to start looking into this further. I agreed that he should start looking into retirement and perhaps look for something part-time that was not quite as stressful as being a criminal defense attorney. He also mentioned that he wanted to purchase a pickup truck so he could haul his bicycle around easier when he went on trail rides and that I could take his SUV that seated eight passengers with our growing family of grandchildren. We now had four, and both daughters wanted more children! I said we should look into it when we got back and things settled down.

We arrived at our hotel at Union Square, checked in, were handed our room keys, and proceeded to our room. We were right across from Lefty O' Doul's, and I could not wait to go and have a Bloody Mary and get this party started. Marty was tired and wanted to take a nap first. I said to go ahead and I would come back after having a cocktail. He didn't want me to go out alone and decided to join me. We both had Bloody Marys and took a selfie together, which, unbeknownst to me, would be our last picture together. I had another Bloody Mary, and he had a double Maker's Mark. It was time to head back to our room and begin getting ready to meet his brother and new girlfriend. We Uber'd over to the restaurant and had cocktails while waiting for his brother and girlfriend to show up. They called and said they were running late, so we had another cocktail. Meanwhile, my younger daughter and family were at the San Francisco Zoo. I called her and asked her if they wanted to join us after for dinner, and they agreed.

Finally, Marty's brother and girlfriend arrived, and we were both so happy to see how happy they were together. She was lovely. My daughter and family showed up, and we were seated—six adults, a five-year-old, and a three-month-old.

We laughed and had a great time. After dinner, I was not feeling well at all. I had hoped that by having dinner, it would help with my headache. After adding four drinks with so much anti-inflammatory medication, I felt like I was going to vomit. The last thing I wanted was to ruin it for everyone. I asked my daughter and her husband as we were leaving if they could drop me off at the hotel on her way home. I knew my husband would be so disappointed, but if I continued, I knew what was inevitable. I told him I had to go back to the hotel room and for him to just have fun! I would see him in a while!

I knew he would miss having me there, but it would be worse if I stayed and got sick. They had a lot of catching up to do, and I just needed to go lie down and make the headache go away.

When I arrived back in our room, the only pajamas I had was the pretty nightgown negligee that I had packed. I was cold and that was the last thing I wanted to put on, so what else does a wife do? I found his giant T-shirt, put it on, pulled the covers over me, and called it a night.

At 7:21 p.m., I received a text from him, "At the Tonga Room, are you sure you don't want to join us?" I replied, "No, live it up! I am still recovering from my cold," and fell back asleep. Again, at 9:46 p.m., I received another text from him, but it was all scribbles and did not make sense. I made the assumption that it was just accidental texting. I knew what state he would most likely be in after even more cocktails. We were veterans with going out of town and whooping it up.

Shortly after, I started to feel intense chest pressure, and it woke me up. I could not take a deep breath. I felt like I was suffocating and sat up. I wondered if I was having a heart attack. Would Marty walk in our room and find me dead? I smelled something. It was similar to when someone in the hotel room next door is smoking, but it was not smoke. It smelled like alcohol. It was an odd sensation. It slowly went away, and I dismissed it.

Probably at around 11:30 p.m. my phone rang, but I missed the call. I grabbed my phone and called back. It was Marty's brother, Tom. He said, "This is not good." I instantly assumed that Marty had fallen down, maybe had another dizzy spell or tripped and dislocated his artificial hip or something. Then his brother said, "Here, someone needs to talk to you." I said okay, and then I heard very clearly, "My name is Bob, and I am with the medical examiner's office. Your husband has passed away, and would you like to see him before I take him?"

I felt so sick. Now I really wanted to vomit. I said, "I am on my way right now." I went into the bathroom and threw on my jeans and black sweater, grabbed my purse, and went to get a taxi. Wait, I didn't have any money. Marty always took care of everything for me.

I ran into the hotel bar and asked if there was an ATM nearby. He said yes, it was in the lobby. I ran to back to the lobby. There was no ATM anywhere! I went to the reservation counter and asked where there an ATM, and I was directed to go outside and around the corner. I ran as fast as I could around the corner and found an ATM machine. I then ran back to the hotel entrance and asked for a cab. Up pulls the next cab in line. The cab driver was so happy to have a passenger who was not drunk. "Hey, how is your evening going?" I responded, "Uh, great, can you please drive me to the Mark Hopkins?" As we were driving the three-mile ride, I noticed that the cab had an ATM machine for credit/debit cards, and I thought about all the time that I had wasted running around to find cash. I had not been in a cab in years and was surprised at how modern they had become. To this day, I carry a small amount of cash in my wallet, lesson learned.

We pulled into the parking lot, and there it was—the medical examiner's van that said "City and County of San Francisco Medical Examiner." This was real. I ran inside and could not remember the room number they told me but said I was Mrs. King. The security guard escorted me to the room of Marty's brother. I walked inside, and there was my husband on a gurney, wrapped in a shroud. Being no stranger to seeing shrouds, I walked over and unzipped it and just looked at my handsome husband. I kissed his cheek. He hated having his face touched. It would have been foreign for me to run my fingers through his hair and feel the outline of his face. I looked closer and could see that his lips and neck were swollen. Hey, wait a minute, he had had an allergic reaction! He did not have his EpiPen with him! I told the attendant from the medical examiner's office that I believed he had an allergic reaction and asked his brother what he ate after I left. He had nothing to eat after dinner, just a few more cocktails, and I was stumped…what happened? I asked the attendant from the medical examiner's if he would like a list that I had kept of Marty's past allergic reactions and the treatments that we did after each event, and he was given a copy from my Notes section on my iPhone. He then handed me Marty's personal belongings, his iWatch, his cell phone, his USC national championship ring, and his wallet.

I asked who found him, and apparently, someone had walked by and saw him unresponsive and notified the front desk. The hotel called 911 and was not able to resuscitate him. They got his personal information from his wallet and looked on the hotel registry for a registered guest by the name of King. They located Marty's brother and went to his room and knocked on the door. His brother had been asleep and said, "Yes, I know Martin King," verified that it was his brother from the forensic pictures, and then called me right away.

According to his brother, after dinner, they went to the Tonga Room for cocktails then walked across the street to Tom's hotel, the Mark Hopkins, and had a nightcap. They decided they wanted to call it a night at around 9:00 p.m. Marty walked his brother and girl-friend to their room and said, "I am going to go back to Diane now, good night!" walked outside the room, closed the door, and collapsed a few feet away. Tom did not hear any noise at all from the fall or from all the commotion a few hours later.

The medical examiner's office took Marty away, and I did not know what to do next. I started shaking uncontrollably. Thoughts were going through my mind about me finally finding my soul mate, the love of my life, and now he was gone forever.

Tom offered for me to stay with them for the night, but I just could not. The hotel arranged a cab for me to return to my hotel. Who would I call to pick me up? My brother was about ten miles away in Orinda, but I did not want to bother him. It was about one in the morning. I knew that I could not call my older daughter. She had a newborn and was recovering from a C-section. In addition, it had been raining, and there were several mudslides with road closures on Highway 17. The only person I could think to call was my other son-in-law. I knew he would be getting up in a few hours to start his work week at the police department. I knew I should not drive; I could not focus. It was such a strange sensation to be so helpless. As an emergency nurse, I was prepared for everything and to handle a crisis with calmness and composure. Why was I shaking so bad?

Okay, I really needed to make that call, and so I did. "Hi, can you call in sick today?"

"Uh, ya, I guess I could, what's up?"

"Marty died," I explained.

"What? Okay, we are on our way right now."

I am lucky he answered his phone. Usually he does not as he gets work calls at all hours. He must have recognized my number and knew something was really wrong. They packed up their three-month-old and five-year-old and started driving to pick me up. I tracked them on my Find My Friends app, and they could not arrive fast enough. I looked around the hotel lobby where I was sitting and wondered what the hotel staff must think I was doing at one in the morning sitting by myself. I could not go to the room alone; I just couldn't do it.

Finally, my daughter and her family arrived and hugged me, and we cried. I gave them the room key and showed them where our room was. I just sat on the bed as they packed everything up. I noticed the room refrigerator. Marty had packed our Hydro Flasks in there so our water would be chilled when we returned to our room. We knew to stay hydrated. I did not even see him do that for us earlier. My son-in-law took our car home, and I rode home in my daughter's car and sat in the passenger seat on that long drive home. As we were leaving San Francisco, we passed some nightclubs, and people were standing outside in miniskirts. It was thirty-seven degrees outside. I was so surprised people really did this. Distracted for a mere second, I told my daughter to look at all the people outside waiting to get in the club!

We drove back to our home, and my older daughter and family were waiting there for us. I was so upset that they had called her. I wanted her to rest. This was too much for her and her new baby! She had turned on the heater and was warming up the house. It was fifty-two degrees inside.

I sat in my chair until the sun came up and rehashed the whole evening. I knew I had to get some sleep at some point. I unpacked for us and put his CPAP machine back on his nightstand, and it still sits there today. After that, I wrote a list of people that needed to be called. Both of my sons-in-law started making the dreaded calls. Next thing I knew, I was told it was on Facebook. I panicked because not all the family knew yet. My daughters took my phone. It was blowing up—texts, e-mails, Facebook Messenger. It was too much for me. All three of my brothers showed up to support me. I am so grateful that we are a close family.

My husband's office partner was called. I knew Marty was scheduled in court in two days. His office partner came to our home carrying three bunches of flowers for us. He was just broken emotionally from the news as well. I went upstairs and got Marty's briefcase and handed his partner the files, and he took care of everything for Marty.

I began making a list of what needed to get done. That day was Sunday. The following day was Martin Luther King's birthday, and the banks would be closed. I converted our dining room table into a very large desk to get all the mounds of paperwork done. Not only did I need to plan the funeral but I also needed to shut down Marty's office and help his clients find representation. His office mate was a godsend and helped make a difficult situation easier. He could not do enough to help me. Marty would have been so thankful, and I know I was.

As I mentioned earlier, my daughters managed my phone and answered my notifications. One message that I received was from one of Marty's elementary school classmates that we had over the previous summer as we had hosted a mini reunion at our home. My younger daughter said, "Mom, I think you should read this."

It said that she had been in contact with Marty after he had passed away and he wanted her to give me a message that he was okay and that, eventually, I would be fine. I texted her back and wanted a lot more information. How did she know that he had passed away? I asked. She said that he had come to her. I had no idea that she was a psychic medium when I met her last summer, not that it would have mattered.

She also said that he struggled emotionally and did not want to leave me but his time was up and he had no choice. I told her that he had an allergic reaction, and she told me that it was not an allergic reaction but a cardiac event. I thought to myself, *Okay, she is not in the medical field. I know what I saw.* I had so many unanswered questions, and she did the best she could to help me get through this.

Without her help, I would be in worse condition and not have gotten through this situation as I did.

Another friend of mine from high school stepped forward and suggested that I talk to a psychic medium that she used when her husband also passed away suddenly and unexpectedly from a skiing accident five years ago. I was unsure about seeking out a psychic medium. I was raised Catholic, and the church does not approve. I gave this a lot of thought and decided to go ahead with her recommendation. I made an appointment, which was months away, and let her know that if there was an earlier cancellation, to please call me. Within a few days, I was able to speak to the psychic medium by phone. I made sure nobody else would be at my home that afternoon to distract me while I took her call. I went into Marty's office upstairs, closed the door, looked out the window, and answered when she phoned at our scheduled time.

When she introduced herself and began speaking, she said that a mother figure was stepping forward and handing me a rose, letting me know that she was with me in spirit and talking to me about my brothers. I stopped her after about five minutes and said, "Wait a minute, I cannot believe that my husband is not breaking down the door to talk to me first." Her response to me was that he was a gentleman and was there and knew that my mother wanted to speak to me first and had stood back so she could get her messages to me first. Then she began speaking about my husband shortly after. As she was speaking, I noticed a flock of wild turkeys coming down my street. They gathered on my front lawn. One of them then jumped onto our roof and stared at me through the window and bobbled his head. I was trying to not look at the turkey because it was so silly and it reminded me of times that Marty was trying to be funny and make me laugh. I kept trying to shoo it away. It was very distracting while I was trying to concentrate. Our family has lived in this home since 1964, and we have seen wild turkeys in our neighborhood. But they have never come into our yard, especially not on our roof.

She continued to talk and let me know he was at peace and calm and that he was so sorry to leave me with such a mess. She also added that it was chaotic when he died. He did not know the person who asked him if he was okay after he passed away. Also, he did not feel any pain. What happened was that he felt dizzy and fell over, as told to me.

I told her about my odd sensation with chest pain around the time of his passing. She told me that was our soul connection. He had to see me one last time before he crossed over.

I asked her about his allergic reaction. She also told me there was no allergic reaction. He described to her that it was like weeds strangulating his aorta in his chest area, which would explain why he was having dizzy spells and an irregular heartbeat occasionally. I still was not convinced. But I did remember Marty telling me on occasion that he felt dizzy.

She also said that he saw our family dog and that the dog saw him and to watch her behavior. She mentioned the dog by name. "Is it Kelly, Kerry, Cami? It is a K-sounding name," she said. Our dog's name is Cami. How would she know that? We talked for about an hour longer, and she let me know how spirit works and what it is like in the afterlife. She said that when spirit speaks to her, it is really fast and she has to listen carefully and will often catch the beginning or end sound of a name. I wrote down what I could as we were speaking so I could remember everything she said. The initial part of our conversation was about my mother, which lasted about five minutes. The remainder of our hour-long call was focused on Marty.

A few days later, I received a call from the medical examiner's office. I had called earlier to ask about the autopsy results and she was finally returning my call. She was so patient with me and my barrage of unanswered questions. She said the cause of death was cardiovascular disease and that he had a buildup of plaque around his aorta! I said, "I don't understand. I saw his face. How can you explain the swollen face, lips, and neck?" She explained that when he had fallen, part of his body was facing down the stairs, and with the lack of circulation, the blood pooled in his upper torso, causing the swollen appearance. She said that his airway was clear. Both of the psychic mediums I spoke with were spot-on. I was stunned.

My daughters were both standing there waiting to hear what I had to say when I hung up from her, in total shock, and I had jotted down notes as I was speaking to her as well. I did not realize that Marty had also fractured his femur on the opposite leg of his hip replacement when he fell. Marty was six feet two inches and large boned. He had to have fallen very hard to fracture his femur. Both of my daughters listened intently as I explained every detail the medical examiner told me.

Meanwhile, people continued to stop by and drop off food for us. Florists were dropping off flowers. It was chaotic at home. I did not leave my chair for three days. I forgot to eat. I still felt like I would vomit. My daughters both made me plates of food and reminded me I had to keep my strength up. It was reminiscent of the days when I was going through chemotherapy. I knew I had to get fluids down at least.

On Tuesday morning, we scheduled a meeting with our parish priest. Marty was well-known in our parish. He was a eucharistic minister as well as a lector at the 7:15 a.m. mass. Marty also helped volunteer at one of the parish annual fund-raisers, the Ghana school project, by barbecuing meat for the fundraising dinner.

The funeral home had called and let me know that his remains were there and available for me to pick up. I drove there, picked them up, and was surprised at how heavy they were. I put the box by our bed, next to his CPAP machine, and it has not moved.

Again, I found my friends circling around me in time of need. My elementary school friends helped organize side dishes for the funeral the following week, along with one of the wives of his high school friend and a longtime law enforcement officer friend's wife. It was such a blessing. We had no idea how many to plan for.

My daughters' friends created Hawaiian shirts for the funeral, similar to what he loved to wear, and had them embroidered saying "Marty's girls." It was so touching. I had two pictures enlarged of him in his happy place—Hanalei Bay, Hawaii, just relaxing in the ocean—and another picture enlarged of him standing near the lagoons near Ko Olina, happy as ever. We got through the funeral. There was standing room only. As we approached the church, my brother asked, "What is going on today? Why are there so many people?" There was a line waiting to get in the church to pay respect to Marty. I do not think he realized how many lives he had touched. I had asked four of his closest friends if they would be able to give a reading, and they happily agreed. After the funeral, we brought home the flowers and pictures. The same two pictures are still in the living room today. The grandchildren give him hugs every time they come over.

Marty would have loved to see people come out of the woodwork to celebrate his life. I am sorry he missed out. He would have enjoyed talking to everyone who came from near and far. I had to catch myself. I wanted to run up and tell him, "Guess who is here!"

Well-wishers stopped by to see how our family was getting through this and brought food for us. I thought I would never cook again. I also thought I would never have parties in our home again like we once did.

My daughters had called my workplace a few days after Marty died and let them know what happened. They were so kind and wanted me to take all the time that I needed. They took up a collection and bought me a gift card to a local restaurant to use for takeout. It was so appreciated. After two weeks' time, I called and let my workplace know that I would like to come back. They let me know that if I needed, while on duty, to take a moment, I should just let them know and they would accommodate. I returned to work and did fine. It was the only place I could go and feel normal again. As chaotic as an emergency department is, it was wonderful to me. When I left work, I did not even hit the exit doors. I was crying uncontrollably and hoped nobody would see me. I was not crying because I feared going home to an empty house. I was crying because this would be my new life.

One day, I was assigned to care for a patient, and he was older, maybe late sixties. He had end-stage pancreatic cancer. He was on hospice care, but his family panicked at home and called 911 to have him brought to the hospital. I went in the room to introduce myself, and it was like déjà vu. This older man looked just like my father did when he was near the end stage of pancreatic cancer—the emaciated, jaundiced look of a person who had given up their fight. I spoke with the family, told them what to expect during their ER visit, how long things might take, etc. Once I answered all their questions, I came out of the room and felt very sad. I began crying, hoping nobody would notice. I still had other patients whom I needed to take care of and had medications to be given to, IVs to start, lab work to draw, and endless charting to do. One of my coworkers, Renee, came up to me, concerned about my dealing with a dying patient and caring for the family and wondering if it was too much for me with the recent death of my husband. I stopped and looked at her and thanked her for her concern. I explained to her this had nothing to do with my husband and further explained it brought back memories of my dad when he was ill in 1999. I was just a traveling shit show. We laughed so hard I was bent over. I needed that.

When I got home, I did not want to leave the house at all. I felt very safe there and surrounded by what was familiar. It took a very long time before I was able to leave during the evening and come home to a dark house alone. Some people who had never been in my circumstance just did not understand why I felt like that. Others were very supportive and came over if they wanted to see me and see how I was doing.

 What was the kindest human gesture that happened to you? Who were the people that helped you the most during your time of need?

CHAPTER 11

Frozen in Time

I WAS IN A CONSTANT state of denial and kept hoping that I would wake up and this would all just be a bad dream. Each day I would wake up hoping; but no, this was my reality. I never went through the anger stage. That does not mean I won't, but it has not happened yet. I tried to bargain with God to just let me talk to him one more time again. Obviously, that is not up to me. I do not have the gift to speak to our loved ones that have crossed over. But I must say that if Marty had his way, he would be watching over our family from above to make sure we are all safe. I would not say that I am depressed or feel lonely. I am kept busy with the grandchildren, work, and helping my daughters. And I always have some project I am working on either at work or at home and have a daily checklist of things I need to get done. Do I feel sad? Absolutely! I have not had one day that I was so sad I could not get out of bed and move on. Choosing to lounge about is another story, lol. I am working through the acceptance phase as I write this book, which has been therapeutic for me knowing that if I can help one person, that is all that matters.

It is normal to experience the five stages of grief, according to Dr. Elisabeth Kübler-Ross. The stages are denial, anger, bargaining, depression, and acceptance. You do not necessarily have to experience these stages in this order, and some stages you may not necessarily experience them at all.

CHAPTER 12

Where Do I Start...

I FEEL SUCH SADNESS THAT we were not able to grow old together. I always told Marty that he would be a cute old man someday. I also felt abandonment; and it was not his fault as we have no guarantees in life, I understand that.

I feel the loss of our ritual Friday night date night. Now I sit at home and read or watch the Hallmark channel by choice. I feel like I am in a constant state of a bad dream and wish this never happened. I have lost a confidant who gave me sound advice and never judged me. I also lost my travel partner. I miss not having someone to dote on and bake pies, cakes, and cookies for on special occasions. I also miss making his favorite dishes, setting the table, and enjoying special dinners with him. We would have great long talks during our coffee and/or cocktail time. I have lost my personal writing editor. He was so good at helping me format a paper. And mostly, I miss the loss of a true best friend.

There are many forms of grief support offered locally within most communities, such as hospital programs, church/spiritual programs, social media platforms, weekly website e-mails, blog spots, and friends/family. Have you reached out to any of these? If not, why?

CHAPTER 13

Taking Care of Myself

DURING THE GRIEVING PROCESS, MANY have felt very tired and lacked energy. I was the opposite of the norm. I would come home from work, change my clothes, and be ready to tackle the next project. I had decided to repaint the entire garage, including the floor, with a high-gloss silver. I even wanted chandeliers! Marty felt that garages are for storing things. I always liked a real clean-looking garage, and now I could do it my way. It took about a week to get everything done by myself. People always comment as they walk by how beautiful the garage looks when I am sitting out there, especially in the summertime. And I politely thank them for their kind words.

I have made the time to sit and have a cup of coffee in the morning, just like we used to do, and also still take the time to take a long leisurely bath, nourishing my body and soul. It is so important to take good care of yourself. I don't sit and enjoy evening cocktails as we once did, but I still do on occasion. It is just not the same anymore, as it once was. I enjoy a nice long walk, writing in my journal, and enjoying downtime.

It was now October, and time had come around for my fortieth high school reunion. I was on the planning committee and busy creating a memory tree for those who had passed away in our class before us, gathering serving platters to use, and planning all the festivities ahead. I looked forward to seeing old, familiar faces from long ago.

We visited, laughed a lot, and socialized; and I made a point to go from table to table to talk to everyone there. By the third table, the question had come up once again from well-meaning classmates whom I had lost contact with over the years, "So what are you doing? Are you married? Do you have kids?" I had never spoken the words "I am a widow" and began tearing up as I explained that I had just lost my husband earlier in the year. I did not realize I was not ready for it. It had been my first social outing without my daughters, who were quick to intervene when I was at a loss for words of explanation. I quietly walked to the bathroom, and it was like I was in high school once again being swarmed by classmates and friends. "Are you okay?" they asked. There was so much support, love, and friendship; but it still stung.

All I wanted to do was leave. I could not leave and have my high school friends gather up all my belongings, the flower arrangements that I created for each table, the memory tree, and the cupcake stands that I brought along. I had to be strong and get through this. I sat and chatted with some girlfriends, watching everyone dance and have a good time, like it was back in the day. Some were trying to get me up to go out and dance and have fun with all of them. I just couldn't. In high school, I danced every dance when we had homecoming and formals and had a great time, but this was so very different. After, we all helped one another get to our cars and load them up, chatting along the way, and I just wanted to get out of there and go home. Most of them kept the party going and continued on at a local bar. I went home and realized I was just not ready for that. I did hear they had a good time and closed the place down. Good for them. Maybe at the next reunion I will too.

Another thing I noticed was that there were a lot of coincidences that occurred through my process of grieving. As I mentioned, at the time of Marty's passing, I was in the middle of planning our high school reunion. One of my daughters had called my girlfriends to let them know what just transpired with Marty, and in turn, she let the others know I would not be able to meet for a while, while I processed what had just occurred. The word spread to my closest classmates; and the phone calls, cards, text messages, e-mails, and flowers began to pour in.

One of the many phone calls was from an old friend from high school who had recently become single whom I hung out with for a period of time our freshman/sophomore year in high school. We were never boyfriend/girlfriend but just really good friends and had a lot of fun and laughs together. I spoke with him briefly on the phone and said that I had to get back to my family as they were waiting for me, and he said, "Well, you have my number now. Please call me anytime," and I said okay. I opened my bedroom door, went downstairs with my family, and looked up at Marty's baseball picture on the mantel. It was the picture of him throwing a fast pitch with an intense and determined look on his face. It then fell off the mantel, hitting the ground, as if Marty did not approve. I said out loud, "Okay, Marty, I understand." I picked up my phone and immediately deleted the phone number from my phone. There was no door open, no breeze, and nobody touched that picture. It just fell. I picked it up and put it back where it had been. Since I met Marty, he has always been the only rooster in this henhouse.

I recalled that the psychic medium whom I spoke to had told me that Marty's number for me was number seven, and she told me to be aware when I would see this number. To validate that she was on track, she asked if my favorite candy was licorice; and I told her yes, it was. Shortly after, I remembered what she said about the number seven when I was driving on the freeway and looking around me. The cars ahead of me on both sides and in front of me had a seven on their license plates. I also remember driving with my brother in the car and telling him this story, and he just listened to me patiently. I said, "Just watch. The next car approaching, I cannot see the plate. It is too far away, but when it does get close enough, let's see if it has a seven on the plate." Sure enough, it did.

A few months after Marty passed away, I agreed to join my daughter and her family on an out-of-town getaway weekend. At hotel check-in, we all received welcome bags that had a variety of goodies in them. I was handed guest bag no. 77 and won the daily prize, a bottle of wine! Inside the goody bag was bottled water, crackers, and licorice, my favorite candy!

As mentioned in an earlier chapter, Marty and I both had pagers in the nineties and would often text each other "143" throughout the day just so we knew that we were thinking about each other. I cannot tell you how many times I have awoken out of a sound sleep, looked at the clock, and it was 1:43 a.m. The message was received.

The funniest time another coincidence happened to me was when I was making salsa recently, using Marty's recipe that he created. (He would laugh and laugh at me in the past when I would try to clean the peppers in running water as I would cough and cough. It was too strong of a smell and irritating to me.) As I was making the salsa, I had to stop because I was coughing so hard. I turned around and happened to look at the clock, and yes, it was 1:43 a.m. I said out loud, "Yes, you think this is just hilarious, don't you?" Cleaning peppers never bothered him, so he usually did this for me when we made the salsa together. I do still make his salsa and share it with everyone. It is worth a coughing spell.

Also worth mentioning here is a story about one of the friends of one of my sons-in-law (another baseball player back in his college days), Alan, who happened to be standing around in their garage with the guys watching a game and having a cold one together. They were all being funny, and Alan was being a wise guy. Marty stopped him in his tracks and shut him down.

After Marty passed away, I asked Alan if he would be interested in installing some chandeliers in my newly renovated chic garage, and he agreed to take on the side job. Being an experienced electrician, he did not expect to get a jolt. He stopped, looked at me, and said, "I think Marty is messing with me!" I just smiled and said, "Well, if he could, he probably would!" He was scratching his head in confusion. I would imagine Marty was grinning from ear to ear from above. He loved all their friends and really enjoyed the humor with these guys.

What coincidences have happened for you? Have you had dreams that you recall that seemed very real?

CHAPTER 14

Showing Gratitude and Celebrating Him

THE PSYCHIC MEDIUMS THAT I have spoken to have unanimously given me the same message but have used different words. They are not all "generalized statements," and most are specific to Marty's situation only and has true meaning to me and are mostly things that others would not know about.

Here are some examples:

- He will always be with me in spirit and that we had true love.
- He had a premonition but dismissed it because he did not want to frighten me.
- He clutched his heart, and it was felt by me, which is why I experienced the chest pain around the time he passed away.
- He felt sorry to leave me in such a mess to deal with everything.
- It is described to me that he is encouraging me to write and will demonstrate as if he is writing things down on paper.

- He struggled with abiding by his needs and keeping on a healthy regimen but now is at peace and calm.
- He is guiding me and wants happiness for me and has a deep sense of gratitude.
- He has concerns that I understand he is with me always. He didn't really "ditch" me.
- He did not want to leave me. He tried to bargain to stay, but his time was up.
- He has a very powerful presence and is strong in spirit.
- He has a good sense of humor and a quick wit.
- We were a match made in heaven.
- I go too fast and need to slow my life down.
- He hears me asking for favors and says "What does she want now?" in a teasing manner.
- He is reunited with his small dog and enjoying time together.

I just do not make this stuff up. I did not volunteer any information to anybody I spoke with, only that my husband died suddenly and unexpectedly. I let them carry the rest of the message to me and validated as we went along.

What I treasure most is when people will come up to me and tell me their favorite memory of Marty or pass along what they have heard others are saying about him. It helps keep his memory alive for me.

This is what I am so thankful for about him:

- He truly understood me, and together we had a synergistic relationship.
- He never judged me or would throw in my face poor decisions that I had made in the past.
- When Marty walked in a room, he had commanding presence; he was not a mousy type man who stood in a corner and was quiet.
- He made me laugh so hard like nobody else and was so smart and had a magnetic personality.

- Lastly, what I am grateful for is that he rarely told me no to anything that I wanted, and if he did on that rare occasion, he had a good reason for it.

 What memories of your loved one have been shared with you by others? How did that make you feel?

CHAPTER 15

Keeping Tradition Alive

I WANTED TO KEEP MARTY'S memory alive, not only for myself but also for my family. A few months after he died, I hosted a birthday party for him in his honor and invited a few of his closest friends over. I created a slideshow with pictures of him on a continuous loop and with music playing in the background. As my daughters and I stood to take a picture together and review it after, we noticed in the background there was a picture of him standing above us, smiling over us. Of the forty-seven pictures that I scanned into the slide, what were the chances of that exact picture of him appearing? I took this as a sign that he is with me all the time, enjoying the good times with all of us, and happy and at peace. I felt good about this.

Marty's friend Len arrived from Southern California to help prepare for the party, as he always did for our big parties. We cooked and made a tray filled with shots of tequila and took time for everyone to tell their favorite Marty story, some stories going back to the 1970s, back in their heyday of being new police officers. Marty also kept in touch with his friends from elementary school, high school, and college days.

In the fall, when the football season began, I also resumed putting his USC flag out on game days. Most of the time he was so proud of the football team and always kept up with what was happening. I still put the games on and geared up by wearing one of our USC sweatshirts, at times feeling frustrated because I didn't understand something that just happened in the game. He would have always been quick to explain—with a story added in, of course.

Another way to keep his memory alive was creating a scholarship for a law student from the law school he attended. When he passed away, I asked that in lieu of flowers, people would consider a donation to the Martin King Scholarship Fund. The screening criteria was that it would be given to a current or former law enforcement officer who was attending law school. We had many donations; and the first year it went to a female officer, and the second year it went to a male officer, both from local police agencies. I was not able to present the scholarship the first year as I was still working through heavy grief and it was only a few weeks after Marty died. By the second year, I was in a better place and attended the ceremony with Marty's law school classmates. We had a lot of laughs, and it was a beautiful evening together, reminiscent of former days.

On his actual birthday, we had a formal family dinner in the dining room and set a place for him and propped his picture up. I prepared one of his favorite meals: smoked brisket, potato salad, garlic bread, and his recipe of Uncle Buck's beans. I propped his enlarged picture in the chair, and we laughed and told stories of the fun times we had.

Do you save a seat at your table for your loved one? Do you leave their picture where it was, or have you moved it? Have you considered creating a memorial wall in your home?

CHAPTER 16

How Do All These Gadgets Work?

As I was cleaning out Marty's beloved cook shack shortly after he died, I came across many of his devices that I had never used and decided not to get rid of anything until I had more time to really take a look at them. I also found many of my beloved spices that had gone missing that I acquired on trips that I had taken along the way. I gathered them up and returned them to the kitchen, shaking my head. I had purchased a nice tin of smoked Spanish paprika while in Spain a few years back, and it was one of the items that had gone missing. I suppose that was used in sausage or dry-rub mix that he was making.

I made the decision to try to make sausage. He had two sausage makers, one was for smaller batches and the other was a restaurant-quality sausage maker that could easily grind about ten pounds within minutes. I started with the small grinder and decided to try the larger one, which was a lot of fun. I can see now why he spent so much time in his cook shack, blasting the music and just having fun. I made Italian sausage, kielbasa, and linguica sausage. I used his packaging machine and created a label. It really was not that easy to figure out, but I had the time to figure it all out and did. I gave my latest creations away to family and friends, and they enjoyed it. The Kielbasa had to be smoked, so I used one of his many smokers.

He also made snack sticks, beef jerky, and summer sausage, but that will be for me to try for another rainy day ahead. I actually have made beef jerky since he passed away but not a wide variety that he would make, such as his spicy version, jalapeño, and teriyaki. I found his recipes on his iPad and created a cookbook for our sons-in-law and wrapped it up and gave it to both of them at his birthday party / celebration of Marty Day last year. I also added in the cookbook some enlarged photos I had taken of him cooking over the years and his final product. They both treasure the cookbook I created for them.

Another change that I made after he passed away was eliminating some of the freezers/refrigerators. For a family of two, we had five refrigerators. It was not cost effective for me alone to have so many. Marty would love to use our membership at the restaurant supply and stock up on beef and pork to grind later when he had time. They were all full, and I gave a lot away, knowing it would not get used in the near future. Now I am down to only the refrigerator/freezer in our kitchen and the barbecue island refrigerator in our backyard that I turn off during the winter months. I just do not use it until then.

Someday, I will pass on to my sons-in-law the remainder of his valued treasures: the sausage-making equipment, the smokers, and his chili-roasting drum that we developed a fondness of while visiting in Sedona.

While visiting in Sedona, we had gone to the local grocery store on a mission to find guajillo peppers. It was from a cookbook we bought in a restaurant called Elote that we absolutely loved while visiting there, and I wanted to replicate the recipe when we got home. We bought the guajillo peppers, packed them in our suitcase, and were looking forward to trying the recipe at home. As we were walking out of the grocery store, someone was roasting peppers outside, and it smelled wonderful. We stopped and talked to them about their machine and asked what else one could cook with it and became intrigued. As a surprise, I ordered one for him when we got home to give him at Christmas! We got great use from it and would purchase hatch chiles every August by the case from our local grocery store. We roasted them, packaged them, and used them all year long. I was afraid to use this device myself because it gets really hot and shoots very large flames that roast the peppers. I still am afraid, and my sons-in-law have agreed that they would roast the peppers for me.

I happened to be in the grocery store weeks later after our Sedona trip and noticed, in the dried-pepper section, that we had guajillo peppers locally. I had to laugh when I told Marty what I discovered.

 What were some of the favorite restaurants that you and your loved one enjoyed? What are your favorite memories?

CHAPTER 17

Hitting the One-Year Mark

I OFTEN WONDER WHAT MARTY is doing. Is he watching football? Is he barbecuing? I am taking this time to be grateful for the time I could spend with him during the past twenty-four years. We shared a lot of great memories, and I could not have accomplished what I did without his support.

One of the biggest challenges that I faced in the last ten years was being the executor of my aunt's estate. This was a seven-year debacle, and I had no idea of the tangled web that I had walked into. Marty gave me great advice initially, and that was to begin documenting all the time that I spent as I had no idea this would become a part-time job.

My aunt had no children and bequeathed the proceeds from her estate to her and her husband's siblings and, in turn, their descendants if they did not survive, which ended up being divided between fourteen beneficiaries. In addition, she had a seven-year clause that her neighbor could continue to operate his auto shop out of her home and large garage. She also owned the home next-door to hers, which was rental property, and the renters were delinquent in back-due rent. I definitely had a challenge on my hands.

I placed the rental property on the market, which was a huge, time-consuming ordeal, and in doing so, the city inspectors, during their home inspection, noticed that a business was being operated in a residential zone right next door to her residence. The city then forced her neighbor to stop the operations of his shop from her residence, which created animosity and a further bumpy road ahead for me.

My aunt's trust clearly stated that this neighbor could occupy the home and garage and was also responsible for paying the taxes and insurance on the property. While following up to ensure this was indeed occurring, I discovered that he was not meeting his obligations and making the payments.

Marty, being the tough guy that he was, was ready to draw up eviction papers for me to have served. I explained to him that it seemed like his approach to this situation was like he was ready to play hardball and that was simply not the approach that I wanted to take. He told me to go ahead and play softball and see where that got me with the irresponsible being. I got the accounts out of arrearages and assumed paying the bills for the trust. I also sought reimbursement, which I patiently waited for, at times three to four months, in order for the trust to be reimbursed; but I persevered until it was done.

Eventually, the very long seven-year debacle was over, and it all worked out with much patience and follow-through that was needed.

Another challenge that I faced that I am forever grateful for is his support as I was working toward my master's degree in nursing. When I began the program in 2005, I was working, helping my aging aunt every other week who lived an hour away, and also taking on the challenge of returning to school in an intense program. This degree meant a lot to me as I knew that someday I would not be able to meet the physical demands of the job that I was currently holding. I was pulling people out of cars that drive up to the ER door; pushing gurneys through the hospital; wrestling with the confused elderly patients who try to get out of bed so they do not fall; and helping to pull people, who cannot help themselves, up in bed. And the walking that was involved—sometimes five to ten miles a day, according to my Fitbit—was a challenge after thirty years of service pounding my feet on a concrete floor. Also, I would be the first in my immediate family to have earned a master's degree, which would have made both of my parents very proud.

One of the funniest memories of us together was when I entered my apple pie into the county fair contest. When we went to see the results, I realized that I won first prize! I asked him if he could join me for the awards ceremony, and he proudly accepted. To hear him describe the event was quite a different story than how I perceived it. He described the story as watching me walk up to pick up my trophy and all the gray-haired old ladies were trying to hit me with their canes because I won. I do not recall seeing gray-haired old ladies with canes nor did anyone take a swing at me. But we laughed and enjoyed the moment.

I entered my pie recipe in another contest a few years later at the Fairmont Hotel and, again, took first prize. My award was winning eight tickets to their Thanksgiving brunch and a set of Emile Henry bakeware pans. To this day, we have returned for their fabulous brunch annually but not on Thanksgiving. We go on Easter, and it is simply beautiful with all the stunning floral arrangements, elegant displays of food, extravagant chocolate displays, and impeccable service. Marty loved seafood, and that was always his first stop. We always loved family gatherings and spending time together.

Which family members / friends would you imagine your loved one spending time with now? Can you imagine their glorious reunion together? What would they be saying?

CHAPTER 18

The Solo Traveler

MARTY WAS NOT MUCH OF a traveler. He did not enjoy traveling outside the Unites States, and that was okay. He never minded if I wanted to travel and was happy to stay home, watch our pets, and keep the house safe. My daughters and I traveled to England and France, and Marty and I kept in touch daily with stories of our adventures and mishaps. We also traveled to Italy, Spain, and Morocco and brought him home a fez hat.

After Marty passed away, a year later, I wanted to go on a tour of Northern Italy. My well-traveled neighbor who was married to a former Pan Am pilot suggested that I look into Perillo Tours. Her husband had flown chartered aircraft for this company on occasion and was impressed with their service to their customers.

I bit the bullet and decided that I would do this solo. Because I have already toured Rome, I wanted to bypass the first few days and visit Positano and Capri. A very close friend of mine and her husband agreed to meet me in Positano and travel with me to Capri. We had a fabulous time and really enjoyed the breathtaking scenery. They continued on to travel elsewhere, and I met up with my tour group in Bologna and proceeded from there. When I checked in to the hotel, the tour guide was there cheerfully greeting me; it was a warm welcome. She let me know that we would be meeting in a few hours for dinner in the restaurant.

I found my room, got settled, and took a brief nap. I freshened up and met my new friends whom I would be spending the next week with at dinner. I was seated at a table of all married couples, and I was odd man out. The seventh seat at the table, just great. Everyone was so kind, welcoming, and nice and did not ask any awkward questions of me. Just the basic "Where are you from?" and general inquisitive questions. Nobody asked me where my husband was, and I so appreciated that. Dinner was fantastic, and they served a pasta dish that I had never seen called trofie pasta with fresh pesto that was very flavorful. After dinner, I walked back to my room, crying. It was a similar sensation of my high school reunion when I could not stop sobbing. I missed being a couple.

The next morning, I joined our group of forty for breakfast. It was free seating, and I noticed two women sitting together. I thought I had hit the jackpot, whew! What a relief it was to me. I asked them if I might join them, and they were happy to have me. Again, they did not ask me where my husband was. I was so relieved. I continued to have breakfast with these ladies every day for the rest of our trip. I did not share that I was a recent widow until the last day. I just did not think I could explain without crying, and I did end up crying as I explained my story to them eventually. They were so kind and told me they were also widows. They both live on the East Coast, and I have stayed in touch with them.

When we toured the gelato factory, they asked for volunteers to help make gelato. Nobody was coming forward, so I did. Slowly, others stepped forward to volunteer also. It was fun, and we learned a lot. We also toured a Parma ham factory and a Parmigiana-Reggiano cheese factory. The towns we visited were Portofino; Cinque Terre; Venice; Lake Como; and Lugano, Switzerland. I found the trofie pasta while we were in the Ligurian region of Italy and wanted to bring some home. I rethought my luggage situation and knew it would be broken into several pieces by the time I arrived home. I had already purchased many souvenirs and was running out of room.

On our last evening together, several people had asked to stay in touch and shared e-mails. I offered to create a private Facebook page to share pictures and stories. It was one of the best trips that I had ever taken, and we are still in touch. We are tentatively planning an upcoming trip to Southern Italy with Perillo Tours in a year or two. Interestingly, in our group of forty, five of us were nurses.

I could not wait to recreate the pasta dish that was served to us. I had gone to five stores in an attempt to find trofie past without any luck. I found it on Amazon and was excited to have the friends that met me in Positano over for dinner and serve it for them along with homemade pistachio gelato. As luck would have it, I found it locally, months later, at our local Italian winery in town. Again, I found recipe ingredients locally that I was not aware of.

When I ventured out with my family for my first trip to our favorite vacation spot—Hawaii—I decided to bring along Marty's ashes to spread. My son-in-law helped me, and we had a mai tai in his honor afterward. Since that time, I have made it a tradition to bring part of him with me on vacation and spread his ashes in very beautiful places around the world. Parts of Marty are now in Maui, Honolulu, Kauai, Kona, Niagara Falls, Bourbon Street, Lake Tahoe, Capri, Sedona, Palm Springs, and who knows where he is going next? A part of him comes with me everywhere. He is in a seal-proof-secured container in my purse.

What have you changed in your life that your loved one would be excited about for you?

CHAPTER 19

Ditched for Good?

WE STARTED OFF THIS RELATIONSHIP with me under the false impression that I was ditched in Vegas, but really, did you just truly ditch me for good?

Marty loved Las Vegas and would often go with his friend Patrick when he lived in Southern California and play video keno in the casino. They could visit for hours just playing. Patrick has truly been a great support, and I have called him several times since Marty passed on and vice versa. He recently became the mayor of his town, and I wish that Marty could be here to celebrate his triumph with him.

I know Marty did not want to leave the physical world and leave me. He was always so doting and caring and would be concerned if I didn't answer the phone. If I was busy, he would repeatedly call my cell phone then call the house phone and so on. I'd finally have to text him to get him to stop. The same applies to his real-life situation. I am sure he struggled emotionally when his time was up. He always watched over me, and if he could from above, he would.

I remember driving down a side street one day and recalling a funny event and talking out loud as if Marty was there next to me and laughing as if he was sitting right there. Hey, wait a minute, he was not right there, and if someone saw me, they would think I had lost my mind! I looked around, and there was nobody in sight. It felt good to laugh, and it did actually feel like he was there laughing with me.

I clearly remember the first time that I laughed really hard after he was gone. The "Marty's girls" bunch had brought a potluck dinner over for all of us and to check in on me and try to cheer me up. A few months had lapsed when they arrived, and it was mostly sadness around this home since he died. Here they came, one by one, taking over the kitchen and setting up their baked potato bar and all the accoutrements along with a delicious fresh salad for dinner. I just sat on the couch and watched them. Next thing I know they are happily eating, talking about their day, and joining me in our living room. As they started talking about funny incidents and events, I, too, found myself joining in and laughing…wait, did I just laugh out loud? It was so foreign for me to feel happiness and enjoy laughing after months of sadness and tears. I cannot thank them enough for that moment and for reminding me that this intense sadness will not go on forever—I can laugh again.

 When was the first time that you truly laughed hard after your loss? How did it make you feel? Surprised?

CHAPTER 20

What Has Helped / What Has Not

ONE OF THE THINGS THAT has helped me was recalling how the females in my family dealt with loss. I am speaking of my aunt and my mother. My mom stayed as strong as she could, under the circumstances. She had no financial worries and was able to stay in our family home. Growing up, she led a charmed lifestyle and did not work outside the house. Her focus was solely on her family, and she was dependent on my father for financial support. She never handled the finances or managed contractors performing work around their home until he passed away. She struggled more adjusting to this new role for her as they were married for almost fifty years. When my father passed away, she became ill shortly after and died within two years of his passing.

My aunt was a workhorse. She worked in the payroll department at Stanford University Medical Center and retired after thirty years of service. She was great with numbers. She also did payroll for her husband's business. When my uncle passed away many years ago, I really admired how my aunt kept on with her schedule. Every day she had a routine: bowling twice a week, volunteering at the hospital, and making time for hair day and shopping/banking/errands day. I never saw her crying or saddened. She held her head up high and kept going strong. I told her one day as I picked her up to run errands with her how proud of her I was. She had no idea that I was observant of her actions. "You have never told me that before," she replied. I think, sometimes, we need to let people know more often how proud they make us, even the little things.

I enjoyed cooking with my husband. I was so proud of him, and we were a great team together. I miss that. He suggested a few years back that I take a class in food safety in the event we wanted to start a side business in catering someday. I have maintained my certification in the event I ever wanted to use that in some capacity later on. An opportunity came up with a small company that helped get home cooks certified to create meals in their own home for purchase, and they took a small percentage of the profit.

I convinced my daughters to help me and promised them both they could have all the profit. I created approximately thirty meal plans, kept myself busy creating shopping lists, photographed food pictures, and was ready to open shop. I advertised via Facebook locally, and each week was a sellout. It was a lot of work, but it was also a lot of fun and fulfilling. I met some great people and got mostly five-star reviews. I tried to make it fun and would create a meal theme. For example, on Valentine's Day, I added in a red candle and candleholder in their meal kit.

I reached completely out of my comfort zone and opened Marty's recipe books. I taught myself how to smoke a brisket and cook smoked ribs on his Traeger and was waiting for an earthquake to happen. The Traeger company made it so easy for me to call with basic questions. As trivial as my questions were, they were patient and calm and understanding with me.

Reflecting on the one time that Marty attempted to teach me how to use the Traeger smoker, I had forgotten to check the pellets and had run the auger dry. He was so mad at me. I happily continued to let him be the barbecue master after that. I did not make that same mistake ever again since I have taken up his hobby. I am glad I had that learning opportunity while he was here to rectify my mistake.

When legislation changed the law about eight months into the year, we had to end our endeavor. I had my groupies, and they were so disappointed and wanted me to continue. They were willing to purchase home-cooked meals from me without the parent company being involved. I declined and hope to resume someday in some capacity. I received a lot of joy visiting with my customers and observed them so very happy to receive some food made with love and healthy for their families.

Imagine what your loved one might be doing right now, free of worldly obligations. What were your loved one's hobbies or pastimes?

CHAPTER 21

Taking the Time I Need

I RECEIVE A LOT OF invitations to connect with friends and have dinner or go to paint night or travel together, but many times, I just want to be alone. And it is okay to say no.

I would not say that I am an introvert, but at times, it feels good to be alone. I have never lived alone by myself, and I must say, I like it. Of course, if I had the opportunity to have my previous lifestyle back, I would take it; but I know that is not a reality. If I leave dishes in the sink or clothes lying around, it just does not matter.

I don't think I have ever spent a day since my teenage years walking around in my pajamas all day, but here I am entering my sixth decade and rocking it. I plan blocks of time now for me with nothing on my agenda, which was unheard of before. I'll glance at the clock in disbelief at where the time has gone. Long leisurely baths, home facials, watching the Hallmark channel, and sleeping in are my new favorite pastimes.

Often, if I am making a big meal, I'll set some aside and bring it to an elderly neighbor who does not cook any more, and she appreciates it. Just sitting with her and having a cup of tea means a lot to her and me too.

Don't forget to allow time for yourself. It is okay to say no, even if you just want to be alone and process your grief.

CHAPTER 22

Resetting Goals

WHEN MARTY WAS ALIVE, I would make his honey-do lists. He hated it, but things needed to get done. I usually did this when I would be at work on the weekends and he had the weekend to himself. Just to be funny, he would read it and then tear it up just to push my buttons. He actually always followed through and would do a great job, often better than I would have done.

One day, I thought to myself, *Why should I stop making lists for him?* I would sit back and imagine what it would be like when, eventually, I get to see him again.

I got my pen and paper out and started writing. At the top of the list was for him to find us the most spectacular beach that we could sit at for hours and just enjoy each other's company. We did do this together while we were in Hawaii and also in Mexico. We would pack our collapsible cooler and whatever we were drinking and just sit for hours, enjoying the view. While we were in Hawaii, our question of the day was whether we would sit by the pool or sit by the beach; and often we did both. But hands down, it was our beach day that was our favorite.

Second, we often ordered the drink of the day at happy hour, which was usually a fruity rum concoction of some sort. My favorite that he would recreate was something he named the electric smurf, which had rum, pineapple juice, blue curaçao, and vodka. I have tried to make it myself, and it is just not the same. We even brought home the heavy Hawaiian mai tai glasses to recreate the memory. Marty was good for about one drink, and then he would switch to either tequila or Maker's Mark. Of course, this was before he had to watch his sugar intake. He was not a fan of what he called fufu drinks but went along with it for me.

I also asked on my list for him to find a dress for me that he thought I would look beautiful in for our perfect evening, complete with matching jewelry. I fondly remember going out to dinner with him in Reno and the waiter commenting to us how he did not see couples dress up that much anymore and how nice it was to see someone take the time to get dressed up. That made me feel good, and I have since always tried to look nice for Marty when we went out.

Of course, since I was putting my requests in, I had to include finding the perfect massage, nice and relaxing, and a facial to help make my skin glow for our perfect evening. I left the mani-pedi off the list. I didn't want to push it.

I also asked him to create a song playlist for us—as he always did when we had a party and he would hook up his iPhone to his elaborate outdoor stereo system—of our favorite songs. I am sure at the top of his list would be the song "Unforgettable" by Nat King Cole, which was our song. And I would be remiss if I did not mention another song that we always played at our annual Mardi Gras party. It was "Papa Thibodeaux" by Eddy Raven. Whenever it played, no matter where we were standing at the party or what we were doing, we would find each other and start dancing together. Even our granddaughter joined in during our last Mardi Gras party. It was hilarious, and we had fun and didn't have a care in the world at that time.

I also put on my list for him to make my favorite dinner. He had it down and knew exactly how I liked it prepared. My favorite dinner is tacos, and he knew which toppings I liked best and made that for me at least once a month, mostly on the weekends that I had to work.

I am sure the list will continue to grow as time goes on.

Consider making a honey-do list for your loved one. If they were able, what would you write on their list?

CHAPTER 23

Oh My! All These Grandchildren!

WHEN MARTY DIED, WE HAD four Grandchildren, and he absolutely adored all of them. He always made a point of coming to the hospital when the girls delivered their babies and brought them something he thought would be special, which was the Hawaiian hula dogs from a local store. We laughed and talked about the fun that we had when we discovered the Hawaiian hula dog store in Kauai and what a great trip that we all had together.

My daughters have since had two more baby boys who never got the chance to meet Marty, but we are keeping him alive around our home with pictures and reminders to give him a hug. We ask them often, "Who is this?" They laugh and say, "It's Grandpa!" He would have treasured this.

Our oldest grandchild remembers him clearly and says she, too, misses him. They were buddies. He kept a picture of them floating in the pool together in his office.

My fondest memory of the grandchildren and Marty together is when we rented a beach house for his birthday. We preplanned our menu, prepped the food at home, loaded up the coolers, and headed toward the beach. When we got there, we got ourselves situated, and the hunt was on with the grandkids and all looking for seashells together. We brought back so many treasures and really had a nice walk on the beach. While I was making a salad inside, I saw someone walk by and stop and talk to him for a really long time. I finished making our salad and went outside to join the conversation. There Marty had been, minding his own business, when someone said to him, "Hey, I know you!" And it turned out that his childhood friend, whom he had not seen in years, lived a few houses away. I could not have planned his birthday better! It was so heartwarming for him to see his childhood friend again. I would have loved to know him as a young boy.

We had a nightly party at the beach house and invited different groups of friends each night. We woke up to the sounds of the waves crashing and wished we had done this sooner in our lives. It was spectacular, and we could not wait to do it again the following year and make it a tradition for his birthday annually.

Marty and I had started many years ago of taking Christmas card pictures together, and when we started having grandchildren, we began including them in our pictures. Now our Christmas cards consist of all the grandchildren circled around me. Of course, they are not all looking at the camera picture-perfect, kind of like herding cats, but it describes who we really are as a family.

We will continue to keep his memory alive as he was a wonderful, loving grandfather and always took the time to talk to his grandchildren and play with them.

If you could gather up your family and/or friends for a vacation, where would you go and why? What would you do there when you arrive? What would be the first thing that you would like to do?

CHAPTER 24

Dealing with Setbacks

ABOUT EIGHT MONTHS AFTER MARTY'S death, I came home from working my weekend, and it was Sunday night at about eight when my phone rang. It was my youngest brother calling me. I answered and listened quietly. "I have had this cough and went to the clinic to see if I could get something to help me get better. They took a chest x-ray and found a mass on my lung, and I am supposed to follow up tomorrow with an oncologist." I told him I would be there with him tomorrow. I know the feeling of getting a cancer diagnosis. I had the advantage of not only being on the receiving end of that conversation but also understanding the terminology as it was explained to a patient. Because the subject matter is so intense, one does not hear everything that is said clearly.

I quickly arranged for my daughter to help care for my dogs and planned to get up early to make it in time to my brother's appointment two hours away. I asked him if it was okay if I asked some tough questions of the doctor, and he gave me his permission. I introduced myself to the doctor and told him of my occupation so that the oncologist knew that I was familiar with medical terminology. I listened quietly and took notes as he was speaking. When he was done explaining, I asked what the five-year survivability rate was and if the hospital that he was on staff at had a specialized unit for oncology patients and what resources did their hospital provide. With sepsis being a huge concern, I had to ask these questions. He answered my questions as honestly as he could, and we thanked him.

Based on his answers, we decided to get a second opinion. I could not have been happier with the second opinion. The cancer center offered a specialized infusion center (or as my brother referred to it, the confusion center); an entire staff that offered social workers, spiritual advisers, stress-reduction classes, acupuncture; and most importantly, I felt comfortable about leaving my brother in their hands. I cannot say I had that gut instinct with the first opinion.

Treatments started right away, and I went to visit as often as I could. My brother felt tired and had a lack of energy, which was to be expected. I made my mom's special cakes, and we talked about the good times and had a lot of fun. We took a lot of pictures together as a family, and I think it made him feel loved. It was nice that we all banded together once again.

He fought cancer for fourteen months. During this time he had asked that we not mention his diagnosis as he wanted it to be kept private. Until the end, our entire family kept our promise. So many extended family members/friends were upset with us for not sharing the information; but it was the last thing we could do for my brother, and we did.

When I went to Italy and then flew back into San Francisco International Airport, he was the first person that I called. I brought him home a rosary from St. Mark's Cathedral in Venice and could not wait to tell him about it. I told him that I would bring it to him the following weekend. He was excited about it. He also shared with me that they had placed him in hospice care. He explained to me that it was because he needed to be in their care to qualify for a study that his oncologist wanted him to participate in. I did not want to sound alarmed but told him I thought that sounded great. My brothers and I met the following weekend at his home and just spent quality time with him visiting. He enjoyed our company and thanked us for coming to visit him.

I had just finished working my weekend on duty at the hospital. After my shift, our family was meeting at the local sports complex to celebrate my granddaughter's birthday at her roller-skating party with her friends and classmates. We had been busy planning a theme party, baking cupcakes, and preparing the goody bags to distribute the day before the party; and we all looked forward to some fun that day. We all had a great time. After the skating party, I was trying to talk both of my daughters and their families into going with me to the local Elks Lodge to celebrate Oktoberfest as they were preparing an authentic German dinner complete with all the trimmings and our favorite German band was playing that night. I was successful in talking them into going, and we had a fun evening together enjoying German music, authentic food, and meeting up with other families that we knew.

I came home, pulled into our garage, and shut my car off. As I was gathering my purse, my cell phone began ringing. It was my brother's wife calling with a nervous voice, telling me that something was really wrong with my brother's breathing and that she thought I should come as soon as I could. I told her I would be there as quickly as I could. I went into the house, got my dogs settled, got back in the car, and drove to their home two hours away. I did not bring pajamas, a toothbrush, fresh clothing, or cosmetics. I just needed to get there quickly.

While driving there, she called again to let me know that my brother had stopped breathing and had passed away. I remained as calm as I could be and asked her to please not let him be removed yet from their home. I just wanted to see him and know that he had passed peacefully. I finally arrived and went right away to my brother. He had a calm look on his face. It appeared that he was not in any pain and did go peacefully. I looked down at his hands, which were by his side. They were flat and not clenched as if he had been in pain prior to his passing. I thanked God that he had let my brother go with dignity in his home with his beloved wife and dog by his side and with the television on in the background while watching a football game.

His wife and I sat and talked for a long time. I asked her if she wanted to take a clip of his hair before the funeral home attendants picked him up. She thought it was a great idea and proceeded to get the scissors and clip his hair in the front. I said, "Wait a minute! Please cut it from the back." I had instant flashbacks of me cutting his hair in my teenage years and telling him I would do a good job but accidentally cutting a chunk of hair with the clippers, which caused him to wear a hat for weeks due to my idea of a future budding career as a hairdresser. We laughed when I told her the story, and she is forever grateful that she has a lock of his hair.

She suggested we do a shot of fireball on his behalf. I agreed, and we sat in the living room, continuing to reminisce. I told her that I would not leave her alone and that I would stay with her until others could arrive. By this time, it was about 11:00 p.m. I slept in my clothes; and when more friends and family showed up the next morning, I felt comfortable going home as she would not be alone.

I felt her sadness and my sadness of losing the first of our siblings, the youngest of us, at age fifty-three. All the emotions flooded back into my memory of how I felt when my husband died, and my heart ached for her sadness. I felt a setback and intense sadness. I know she did also. I told her to take her time grieving. We are all different and process it differently. People have made insensitive remarks to me about moving forward, and it is unwelcome. We deal with such a life-changing event on our own time frame.

It is completely normal to feel at times that you are not progressing in your grief process and that you are stuck. Take all the time you need to get better. There is no time limit. Ignore the comments if any are made about letting go, and take all the time you need.

CHAPTER 25

Growth and the Second-Year Mark

I MAKE SURE THAT I take the time each day to be thankful for what I still do have. I have come to the realization that I am not going to wake up from a really bad dream and everything will be back to normal again for us. This is my new reality, and it is not going to go away. What has been the most difficult aspect of grieving for me to grasp is that Marty is not going to call me tomorrow or the next day or the day after that. No matter where in the world I or he was, we spoke daily; and on most occasions, it was several times a day. Even when I was working as a ship nurse for Holland America cruise line, I borrowed a satellite telephone from a friend so that I could speak to Marty daily while in the Baltic Sea region, Scandinavia, and even when in Russia. We always made the time, no matter what.

It is surreal how life is so fragile, talking daily to each other and then being silenced forever. I have hoped for dreams that I could have of us having conversations together again, which have not happened yet. Perhaps the grief is still too strong. The only dream that I recall having was with him sitting in our kitchen at our table. He was just sitting quietly, saying nothing. I remember hugging him and looking intently in his eyes to see if it was really him, and then I woke up. I felt sad because I realized how much I miss him.

It has been quite a journey; and I am still working through it, one day at a time. I occasionally look back as a reminder to myself of the stages that I worked through in the process of grieving. I will never get over this, but I will get through this. Of course, I can do this.

 What dreams have you had, if any? How did you feel when you recalled your dream?

About the Author

DIANE KING IS A NORTHERN California native and works as a registered nurse in a community hospital in the emergency department. Diane has earned her master's degree in nursing with a focus on nursing education and helps organize trainings at her workplace. Diane's husband passed away suddenly and unexpectedly in January 2017 from sudden cardiac arrest. Her hopes in the publica-

tion of this book is that it will help others understand and learn in a healthy manner how to deal with the profound lesson of losing a loved one. Diane also shares her experience dealing with life's adversities. At the end of each chapter, she offers suggestions that might help others who have experienced losing a loved one. Diane is resilient and a thirty-year cancer survivor. Her hobbies include worldwide travel, gardening, walking her dogs, scrapbooking, and volunteering. Diane has two married daughters: one is also an emergency department nurse, and the other is a business marketing consultant. Diane helps care for her six grandchildren in her spare time.